A Celebration of Children

A Celebration of Children

Edith Schaeffer

Foreword by
Ruth Bell Graham
and
Gigi Graham Tchividjian

A Raven's Ridge Book

Baker Books
A Division of Baker Book House Co
Grand Rapids, Michigan 49516

Published by Raven's Ridge Books
an imprint of Baker Book House Company
P.O. Box 6287, Grand Rapids, MI 49516-6287

The majority of material presented in this book has been excerpted and reorganized from *What Is a Family?*, *Common Sense Christian Living*, and *Ten Things Parents Must Teach Their Children*.

Printed in the United States of America

Library of Congress Cataloging-in-Publication Data

Schaeffer, Edith.
   A celebration of children / Edith Schaeffer ; foreword by
Ruth Bell Graham and Gigi Graham Tchividjian.
     p.   cm.
   ISBN 0-8010-1193-0 (cloth)
   1. Parent and child. 2. Parent and child—Religious aspects.
3. Family. 4. Family—Religious life. 5. Children. I. Title.
HQ755.85.S334 2000
649'.1—dc21   99-089651

Edith Schaeffer would like to thank Stephen Griffith, Bonnie Church, Amy Nemecek, Brian Brunsting, and Mary Wenger for their help in putting together this book.

For current information about all releases from Baker Book House, visit our web site:
     http://www.bakerbooks.com

Interior design by Brian Brunsting

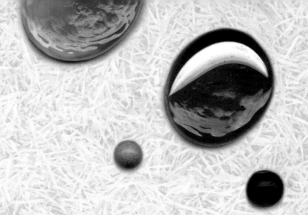

Edith Schaeffer, wife of the late Dr. Francis Schaeffer, is cofounder with her husband of L'Abri Fellowship, an international Christian community and study center that has ministered to thousands of people searching for answers to life's toughest questions. As a best-selling author and speaker, her message of commonsense Christianity has touched hundreds of thousands of lives.

Other books by Edith Schaeffer:

Affliction
A Celebration of Marriage
Commonsense Christian Living
Ten Things Parents Must Teach Their Children
What Is a Family?

More information is available on both Francis and Edith Schaeffer's books at the web site:
　　http://www.sgriffith.com/authors/schaeffer/index.html

Contents

Foreword

Edith Schaeffer is one of my favorite people. Personally she is a delight, and I have found her writing a true reflection of herself. Not only a delight but informative and inspirational.

It is a pleasure to recommend this book, *A Celebration of Children*, to you.

—Ruth Bell Graham

My husband was born in the village next to where Edith and Francis Schaeffer lived in the Swiss Alps. For many years after our marriage, I was able to spend much of my time in this Alpine village.

I have warm, detailed memories of attending church on Sunday in the little L'Abri chapel nestled in a field which hugged the side of the mountain overlooking the majestic snow-covered Alps beyond.

No matter what the temperature outside, it was always warm in the chapel. Many bodies, from many countries, crowded together to listen to Dr. Schaeffer expound Scripture. Deep truths were taught, and even as an adult I often found his messages challenging to comprehend.

But my most vivid memory of church at L'Abri was observing Edith Schaeffer, sitting in the back, surrounded by her grandchildren. There on the long bench, with pen and notebook, she would painstakingly illustrate each sermon for the children. What came out of those Sundays, and what comes out of this book—*A Celebration of Children*—is Edith Schaeffer's great love for children and her deep desire that children, as well as adults, know truth.

Edith Schaeffer has always taken seriously God's instruction to raise up children to know and follow Him. Jesus said, "Let the little children come to me," and Edith has done her best to bring as many as possible to Him.

—Gigi Graham Tchividjian

Introduction

As a mother, grandmother, and great-grandmother, I can look back over many years of life and wish I had done things differently at many times. I see my life in chapters, or blocks of time. I realize that no chapter can be erased, no block can be torn out and built again like a house being changed with walls where there were none, new windows, fresh wooden floors. There is no "remodeling" job available to any one of us for the moments or periods of time we regret!

Life has to be lived within the reality of *time*. There is a whole lifetime which is like a complete book, but there are many chapters in life, and sections within those chapters. It *is* possible to make changes in the present and future chapters.

There are choices to be made from hour to hour, from day to day. The choices parents, grandparents, aunts and uncles, friends, and teachers make affect lives, and lives affect history. Choices affect the next generation and must be thought about and considered day after day.

Choices like what?

Choices like having an unbreakable appointment with a small child or children, to sit on the floor and play an appropriate game together, and to take that child on your lap and read a story, maybe over and over again. Choices like putting on some good music and marching around the room to it or giving a little drum or cymbal to the child to keep time with the beat. Choices like giving (if at all financially possible) piano lessons, or lessons on a violin or recorder, by six or seven, if there is a truly pleasant and good teacher available . . . then sitting with the child as he or she practices, living that section of life together. Choices like spreading out paint, paper, scissors, and paste and doing a creative thing with your little ones, rather than considering all adult "appointments" more important.

Not convenient? If your children are to be lifelong friends, you must recognize very early in your life together that the most valuable and precious times will take place when it is *not* convenient. You "need" to be somewhere else! You "have to go."

The words "mother," "father," "mummy," "daddy," "mom," "papa," should be comforting words that conjure up a feeling of "available." The very words that bring a picture of the parents to the children should bring a picture at the same time of a place and persons to run to for help or comfort or just plain understanding!

It is hard to explain even with a small amount of understanding the availability of our God and Heavenly Father who has said, "Come unto me, all ye that labor and are heavy laden, and I will give you rest" to someone who has never known the availability of a human father, grandfather, mother, or grandmother who is ready to listen.

If you are an aunt or uncle, you can provide this kind of availability in some measure. If you have no children related to you, there are so many neglected children in this world whose need of a welcome and listening ear is great. Of course, none of us is infinite, and we can only be a help in a limited way. For our own frustration of the enormity of what is needed compared to our limited time and energy we can be comforted by the fact that only God is infinite and unlimited. Only God can be available at any time of the day and night when we call upon Him for help, wisdom, and comfort.

God has made clear that His children are important to Him and has provided the costly price necessary for Him to have an "open door." That price is beyond anything we can provide for any child we care for. The Father sent His only Son to empty himself of heaven's glory and beauty to live on this earth and then to suffer cruel death for us. That is the price paid for our being able to run to the Father at any minute of the day or night. Can we ever understand the meaning of the word Father? Or how important it is to teach the deepest things by imperfect yet real examples?

To show a reality of love, concern, and availability to our children costs something for each of us. This cannot simply be tacked on as a P.S. to everything we want to do first. Sacrifice is the price the Triune God paid to make it possible for us to approach Him with our praise and our requests. There is always a measure of sacrifice needed for us as parents, grandparents, aunts and uncles, to be open to a child's seeking us.

As you read this book of ideas, perhaps you will find practical ways to do that which you have not thought of before.

I met a brilliant career woman a day or two ago. She has had two marriages, a diversity of experience in many parts of the world, and several involvements in Eastern religions and what the Bible calls the worship of false gods. The wistful longing in this woman's eyes needed no interpretation as she watched my nine-year-old grandchild jump off the bus at the steps of Chalet le Melyer in Huemoz, kiss me, accept a glass of apple juice at our sunny outdoor cafe table, and then breathlessly say, "Good-bye, Mommy might be worrying." The woman expressed her longing eagerness as she said, "I wish I had a child . . . I would like a child more than anything else in the world." She could easily have had a child of that age by now, had her choices been different.

Among other misconceptions about "choice" is the one that no one points out—a piece of time, a section of time, a certain length of time is the price of choice. Time cannot be used over again. Time cannot be taken to the cleaner and brought back as good as new, to be used in another way.

The use of time is a very permanent thing, whether one wants permanency or not! Time moves from the present tense into the past tense very relentlessly . . . a minute, an hour, a day, a week, a year, nine years. There it is. Childhood cannot be used over again for another set of preparation nor a different set of memories. The teenage years cannot be lived over again, but neither can the twenties, nor the thirties.

I am not saying that a career is wrong for a woman. Some women are able to do amazing things

ONE
Our First Home

because of the abundance of energy, efficiency, and talent. They can have both a successful career and be an imaginative homemaker.

It is important to say, however, that the first home of every human being that has ever been born throughout history has been the body of a woman. It is an incredible wonder that needs recognition—that only a woman can be a human being's home for nine months. The word *homemaker* may be applied to a father after the new person is born, but the nine months a human being is growing from conception to birth are spent in the *only* perfect home.

The wistfulness of wanting a nine-year-old to be near, to run home to you, is based on an accompanying wistfulness of wanting to be a home for nine months of a private personal living human being. What a potential is given. However, that possibility exists only for a certain period of time—shorter or longer, depending on the individual woman. This possibility needs protection. Disease and injury can render the body incapable of being a home. Also, conditions such as sterility, which are no fault of the individual woman, may make it impossible for a woman ever to be the home of a human being.

The use of those nine months is a very precious use of time. No career can compare with bringing forth Beethoven or Bach, or Leonardo daVinci or Michelangelo, or Shakespeare, or John Bunyan, or Thomas Edison, or David Livingstone, or Ethel Waters, or Mother Teresa, or Amy Carmichael, or Madame Curie. What could be more fantastic than being the home of another human being you have not met yet? That person may be a great football player, or a girl who will excel in ice skating, or a president of your country, or a scientist who will find a cure for lung cancer. Or that person may be someone who will need your special care because something has gone wrong during the nine months of living in that home that is you. Perhaps excellence in caring in such an imaginative and special way for your handicapped child will blaze the way for other mothers, teachers, and therapists with ideas and successes that will help others. There is an unknown result of the use of those nine months, but there is also an unknown result of the use of that same period of time in a career.

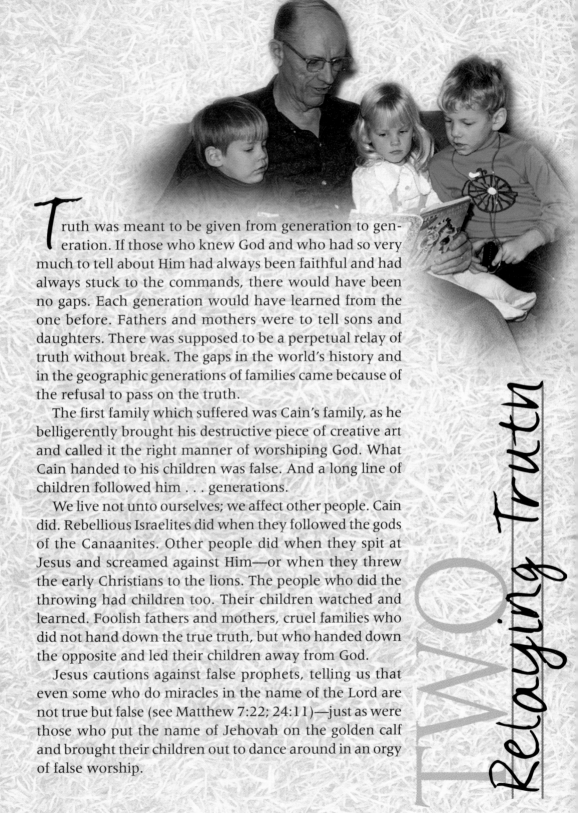

Truth was meant to be given from generation to generation. If those who knew God and who had so very much to tell about Him had always been faithful and had always stuck to the commands, there would have been no gaps. Each generation would have learned from the one before. Fathers and mothers were to tell sons and daughters. There was supposed to be a perpetual relay of truth without break. The gaps in the world's history and in the geographic generations of families came because of the refusal to pass on the truth.

The first family which suffered was Cain's family, as he belligerently brought his destructive piece of creative art and called it the right manner of worshiping God. What Cain handed to his children was false. And a long line of children followed him . . . generations.

We live not unto ourselves; we affect other people. Cain did. Rebellious Israelites did when they followed the gods of the Canaanites. Other people did when they spit at Jesus and screamed against Him—or when they threw the early Christians to the lions. The people who did the throwing had children too. Their children watched and learned. Foolish fathers and mothers, cruel families who did not hand down the true truth, but who handed down the opposite and led their children away from God.

Jesus cautions against false prophets, telling us that even some who do miracles in the name of the Lord are not true but false (see Matthew 7:22; 24:11)—just as were those who put the name of Jehovah on the golden calf and brought their children out to dance around in an orgy of false worship.

TWO   Relaying Truth

Listen to what God says to the children of Israel:

Only be careful, and watch yourselves closely so that you do not forget the things your eyes have seen or let them slip from your heart as long as you live. Teach them to your children and to their children after them. Remember the day you stood before the LORD your God at Horeb, when he said to me, "Assemble the people before me to hear my words so that they may learn to revere me as long as they live in the land and may teach them to their children."

Deuteronomy 4:9–10

How *clear* it is! The truth of the existence and character of God is to be made known to the children and the children's children. We are responsible to make known the wonder of who God is, what God has done, and what God has said and what He has meant to those doing the telling.

God makes it clear in Deuteronomy 6 that parents are also to tell their children to love the Lord their God with all their hearts and souls and all their strength. In chapter 7 verse 9 we are told that God is a faithful God, keeping His covenant of love to a thousand generations of those who love Him and keep His commands. But these thousand generations are meant to *hear* all about God's marvelous creation and the history of His great works from their fathers and mothers. Questions are to be answered as children ask them that they may know the history of what God has done through the ages before. Truth is meant to be relayed and was meant to be relayed through the centuries.

Just so, prayer was meant to be faithfully made for the next generation and the next and the next. Intercession was meant to be a relay—a race in which a stick is passed from one runner to the next. Each new generation was meant to have faithful grandparents, great-grandparents, parents, uncles and aunts—*all* interceding for them.

In the relay of passing truth to the next generation and interceding for the next generation, God alone would be able to trace exactly who dropped the stick, so to speak. Dropping the stick in these crucial relays has made a difference in history. The relay of truth and the relay of intercession are imperatives for your life and mine for present and future history.

The Creator is to be marveled at, and as we walk and talk with our children, the wonders of His creation should be pointed out.

"Look, dear, at that wonderful magnolia tree coming out with creamy, perfect blossoms. Only God could make such a growing thing. Just imagine, it was once a tiny little tree and it grew into a big one. God can make things grow and then produce seeds that are new seeds of the same kind. Isn't He wonderful?"

"Did you hear the bird's song? Listen to it! Imagine God creating birds that could sing like that. He would have those sounds in His mind first, just like a music composer has sounds go through his head when he is writing music for a violin or for a whole orchestra. How great God is!"

"I see the first star! Can you find it? Did you know that there are so many stars that no one can count them? But God knows because He made them, and He made all the complicated things of the whole universe to fit together perfectly."

"Let's play a game about who made what I see. I see Patty's dress." "Mommy made it." "Good for Mommy. She chose the stuff out of a lot of materials and chose a pattern and imagined in her head what it would look like on Patty. Good choice, don't you think?"

"Let's continue the game by picking out other things in this room and telling who made them. Now

THREE *Wonder of creation*

let's tell of a few things only God could make. It's good to think about the greatness of God."

Come back to Deuteronomy.

Hear, O Israel: The LORD our God, the LORD is one. Love the LORD your God with all your heart and with all your soul and with all your strength. These commandments that I give you today are to be upon your hearts. Impress them on your children. Talk about them when you sit at home and when you walk along the road, when you lie down and when you get up.

Deuteronomy 6:4–7

I f you have family prayers at the table, the reading should be fairly short and the prayer time very real. If it is to be prayer, it should not be superficial but actual praying for needs of the family, for people the children ask prayer for—or whose needs you share with them. When children pray at night, they shouldn't be forced to pray, but you should pray with them if they don't want to pray. "Oh, you don't want to pray tonight? That's all right. You can talk to God alone after I've left the room if you want to. He doesn't go out, but He is always here with you and always has the time to listen. I'll pray now, though."

When you pray for cousins or play-mates, people whom the child knows, don't make some sort of pattern for them to follow, but make it real for you. Many a time my children have fallen asleep as I've knelt by their beds praying for the very real needs of the moment.

A child should be sung to before he or she is old enough to know the words—but gradually such words as "Jesus loves me! This I know" will be familiar and happy words connected with Mother's and Daddy's certainty that the words are true.

The singing of hymns and cho-ruses and psalms, songs with hand motions, should be joyous times, around a piano if you have one, banging on triangles for the little ones—and by recorders or violins if you have budding musicians. Marching around while banging on little drums or cymbals, little children should be singing, "Dare to be a Daniel, Dare to stand alone!" They will be enjoying it like mad, but also as time goes on, learning that standing *alone* like Daniel can be very real in their own lives.

Do you have a rocking chair? A sleepy child, a feverish child, a sad child, a child full of fears? A child needing special closeness can't have anything quite like a parent rocking him or her with a quilt thrown around both people, rocking and singing (never mind the voice or the ability to keep a tune):

> Great is Thy faithfulness!
> Great is Thy faithfulness!
> Morning by morning new mercies I see;
> All I have needed Thy hand hath provided.
> Great is Thy faithfulness, Lord, unto me!

There is something you can give your child in hearing the marvelous words of God's promises sung and seeing your faithfulness and love being demonstrated. You are handing the flag of truth to the next generation.

Jesus shows us how gentle we are to be in receiving children, not brushing them away as without importance. The importance of praying for and with the next generation, the value of human beings of a very young age, is sharply demonstrated in Matthew 19:13–14:

> Then little children were brought to Jesus for him to place his hands on them and pray for them. But the disciples rebuked those who brought them. Jesus said, "Let the little children come to me, and do not hinder them, for the kingdom of heaven belongs to such as these."

We are commanded that a part of our growing Christian life is openness to others, that is, hospitality. Now hospitality is often thought of as serving a meal. We think of hospitality as giving someone in our own "circle" a warm welcome.

Think of prayer as another form of hospitality. As with everything we are to do, finiteness makes it impossible to invite the whole city into our space, but we are to include some. Prayer takes time and energy and is a matter of choice. As we each take a notebook and begin writing down

FIVE To Such as These

the names of those for whom we want to intercede, we will soon discover how much choice is involved, and we will worship more deeply our infinite intercessor, the Lord Jesus Christ, who is not limited and does not have to choose which one to pray for today.

That day as Jesus took the little children on His lap and prayed for them, He did not have every child in the world on His lap, because at that time He was truly man as well as truly God. He then could show us, as our example, how we are to give hospitality in prayer for the ones who come to us, into our minds, into our homes.

The point here is that it is imperative to pray for the next generation. Had all the people who should have been interceding for the next generation really been faithful, had true hospitality been given in intercession through the ages for the children coming along, there would have been an enormously different history, it would seem.

Human relationships start at birth and continue to death, whether or not anyone consciously thinks about it. Good or bad human relationships and constructive or destructive human relationships take place at every level of life. Whether people treat people as human beings or machines, people are treating people in some way. Whether people treat everyone as having importance, dignity, significance, or whether people treat others on a sliding scale of importance—everyone is reacting to other people in some way.

A family is a formation center for human relationships. The family is the place where the deep understanding that people are significant, important, worthwhile, with a purpose in life, should be learned at an early age. The family is the place where children should learn that human beings have been made in the image of God and are therefore very special in the universe.

SIX Setting an Example

Parents have been teaching children lessons of how to treat other people, in devastatingly horrible ways or in biblically right ways, whether or not they have ever thought of themselves as teachers. Teaching takes place by example, every minute of every day, for every human being.

The Bible tells of the things which children should be learning at an early age in order to find out how human beings are to treat other human beings—whether they are in the personal family, in God's family, friends, neighbors, or enemies. God gives every basic teaching; guidance by example is supposed to be in line with what the Bible teaches. Teaching should be given and discussed with day-by-day pointing out of where one or another teaching can be practical and where we may have acted contrary to the Bible.

Can parents be perfect? Of course not! Can brothers and sisters be perfect? Of course not! Children should learn from very early that we are all sinners and we all fall into times of misbehaving. Reality in the area of difficulties in human relationships should also be experienced together as well as talked about. Children should know that adults don't always carry out what they should, in keeping with what the Bible teaches them to have as a basic rule of behavior. Children should know that mistakes are made and that parents fall into sin at times. Apologies should be made to small children by their parents. The understanding of what an apology is and what forgiveness is should be a two-way street from the very beginning. Pretending perfection immediately teaches falseness and rationalization of mistakes as the very first lessons.

The understanding of how to deal with and live with human beings takes a lifetime. The fact that progress is to be expected should give a feeling of excitement to the whole relationship within the family, which will naturally spread out beyond the little family to touch other people.

The family is the place where loyalty, dependability, trustworthiness, compassion, sensitivity to others, thoughtfulness, and unselfishness are supposed to take their roots. Someone must take the initiative and use imagination to intentionally teach these things.

There should be family discussions about the centrality of growing relationships being more important than individual points one wants to get across. Criticism of each other may be very necessary at times, but there must be encouraged sensitivity to the fact that the whole point of communication is to have a growing relationship come forth.

Compassion and understanding of what another person needs comes through having been cared for. Anyone who has had the comfort of a little pot of tea, some cookies or toast, or a cup of coffee and some cheese and crackers, or a glass of milk and some fruit brought to him when he was feeling "down" in the midst of a project—then knows how to do the small things for someone else! A family is the place where this kind of care should be so frequently given that it becomes natural to think of the needs of other people.

Love is one of the basic commands which the Bible gives us concerning human relationships. Husbands are to love their wives. Christians are to love each other. People who are in the family of the Lord are to love those who are not believers. Love is the basic ingredient of human relationships which is meant to be taught in the family. The family is the formation center for knowing how to love, how to express love, and what love is all about. We should be expressing love for each other verbally and not be too embarrassed to say, "I love you, Mother"—"I love you, Dad"—"I love you, Son." Children need to grow up in a place where love is freely expressed and becomes a perfectly normal thing to verbalize, just as "What a gorgeous sunset!" is normal to talk about.

Love isn't just happiness in ideal situations with everything going according to daydreams of family life or married life or parent-child closeness and confidences. Love has work to do. Hard and sacrificial work—going on when it would be easy to be provoked and think evil. Love takes imagination and the balance of putting first things first to be taught to young people in the formative years. Day-by-day living in the midst of an outpouring of examples of love is needed through months and years, if love is to be a basic part of the "warp" and "woof" of a person.

Can human love be perfect? No, but it is meant to be worked at through the years, and it is meant to portray something within the family of the love of God for His family. What is a family? A formation center for human relationships.

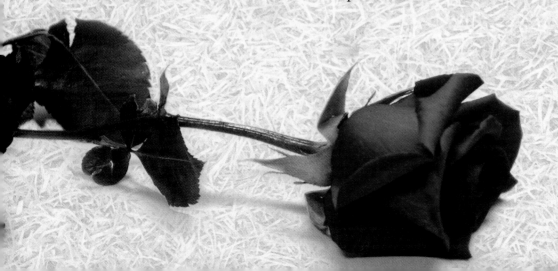

a phone call comes when you are just ready to turn out the light and go to sleep, or when you are halfway out the front door. The person on the other end of the line is your child who will take your time, but whose conversation is a special continuation of your close friendship. You realize that at least a few minutes are essential. To cut this time off would be to lose something precious, not just for the moment but for the reassurance your attention is giving that other family member that you really care.

Naturally, if you are a surgeon running to do an emergency operation, you say so, and your son or daughter will understand as you say, "I'll get back to you as soon as I can." It is the pattern that is important, and the exceptions are easily accepted. If, however, everything else always comes first, your children will feel they are always last in being considered important.

You are just in the midst of writing a chapter of a book, and one of your children comes in and sits on a chair and says, "I have something I need to talk to you about." My feeling is that there is no use writing about life, in any area, unless you are willing to stop writing and live.

EIGHT
Inconvenient moments

Being available at an inconvenient time is part of really living as a mother or father.

Your child begins to talk to you after you've read a story and you are tucking him into bed. Your mind is outlining what you will do next—"I'll do dishes now . . . then I'll do this and the other and so on . . ."—but your child is opening up with a question important to him or her or is about to confide some special thing to you. This moment is not going to come at another time. If you slam the door on this particular use of the next half hour, you are finished with whatever this close moment was going to consist of. That specific time is never to be repeated.

Learn to stop your brain and actions to ask yourself a question: "What is more important? My relationship with this child or getting the child in bed at the right time?" You answer the question by telling yourself, "Stay. Do the dishes later."

Naturally, there are myriad examples of inconvenient times for shared confidences or precious discussion of ideas or accounts of projects that have been completed. Inconvenience is the shared ingredient of a variety of pieces of time. Finding time for communication in the midst of a very heavy schedule is difficult. I would say that the only time I have found for valuable communication with each of the members of my family has been when it has been inconvenient. If you are not willing to stop and take the inconvenient moment, you are not going to have any real communication.

One lesson I tried to teach my children from an early age, repeating over and over again the best explanation I could think of, was the fact that some things must *never* be said, no matter how hot the argument, no matter how angry one becomes, no matter how far one goes in feeling, "I don't care how much I hurt him or her." Some things are too much of a luxury *ever* to say. Some things are too great a price to pay for the momentary satisfaction of cutting the other person down. Some things are like throwing indelible ink on a costly work of art, or smashing a priceless statue just to make a strong point in an argument. Saying certain things is an expense beyond all reason. Proverbs says something in this direction, which applies whether you are a mother or father or child:

> The wise woman builds her house,
>   but with her own hands the foolish one tears hers
>   down.
> A fool's talk brings a rod to his back,
>   but the lips of the wise protect them.
>
> Proverbs 14:1, 3

NINE

Lips of the Wise

What is it that can never be put in words, which can't be erased or forgotten? What is it that is like plucking your own house down, pulling your own family into pieces around your own ears, and creating a ruin of the most precious relationship? It is pulling the rug out at a place where the other person felt there was a solid acceptance and understanding. It is bringing up something from the other person's background which he has no control over and which carries with it painful memories. It is turning the one secure place in all life into a suddenly exposed place of naked attack from which there is no place to run.

At some point in the beginning of a relationship, it is of tremendous importance to decide inside yourself that you will never resort to saying anything about his or her big nose, deformities, psychological fears, or special weaknesses. Naturally it can't be too big a list, but there must be specific areas you rationally decide not to "let wild horses drag out of you." It is possible. It is a restraint that you can inflict upon yourself.

Have you ever broken ribs or badly bruised all muscles in a severe fall directly on your rib cage? I have. It is amazing how suddenly controlled is my coughing. How gentle and limited in volume is my need to cough or sneeze, how controlled my burst of humor—a quiet laugh taking the place of an unlimited guffaw. Immediate pain sets the limit, and the knowledge that more pain will follow gives strength to the power of control. The freedom to cough, sneeze, and laugh becomes too luxurious a freedom, the cost is too great to indulge in, except with firm limits. This is an illustration that we do set ourselves limits in a variety of things, even in areas that seem spontaneous.

Not only must you select the areas with some degree of exactness and shy away from them, but children should be conscious that there is an absolute limit to what can be said to each other.

Say to yourselves and teach your children that there are some things too costly to say, some things that are too cleverly devastating to ever use in trying to get the better of someone. To win in the midst of saying that kind of thing is to lose entirely.

There should be family discussion about the centrality of growing relationships being more important than individual points one wants to get across. Criticism of each other may be very necessary at times, but there must be encouraged sensitivity to the fact that the whole point of communication is to have a growing relationship come forth. If criticism is degenerating into a simple power struggle, one needs to stop and ask, "What is more important, our relationship or convincing him or her that I am right?"

Every discussion in which two people are differing does not need to continue on to the bitter end. There can be a change of subject, an introduction of a pleasant thing such as reading or music or just listening to the other. Children are quick to learn in early childhood how to clear the air by the introduction of a fresh subject, and they ought to be helped, not squashed. There should be open discussion as to how to use precious time together for everyone's benefit and to help the relationship rather than to run headlong into a quarrel.

I am not suggesting a disregard of serious subjects. It isn't that serious subjects need to be avoided in order for relationships to grow—quite the contrary. But that does not rule out consideration and sensitivity in the midst of discussion.

We knew a family in Lausanne several years ago, a mother with a son and daughter who sometimes lived with her in a temporary apartment and went to a day school—or sometimes to a boarding school. Father was an importer/exporter who traveled most of the time around and around the world. When the teenage girl asked, "Dad, why can't you ever be home? Why can't you do less and have some time together with us?" the reply was, "I have to earn enough to have enough to leave for you, your mother, and your brother—so that if I die you'll have enough." This is not exaggerated. That family lived in a temporary situation for years, getting ready for the future which, when it came, would leave only part of the family there to pay the government taxes on inherited income, and they would be without a father.

We all know of families where father and mother work "until we get another car" or "until we pay for this house" or "until we save enough for Johnny to go to college." Months go by, years go by, and the children can have a key worn around their necks or they have a baby-sitter to meet them when they get home from school.

What is important to provide with the work that is being done? There is a need for serious discussion and family prayer together in considering the area of economic things.

Coming now to "family economics"—making a home is one of the primary necessities for having a place and an atmosphere for family life. Read aloud together Laura Ingalls Wilder's book *The Little House in the Big Woods* and others, and your children will be wishing Daddy could build a log cabin himself, shoot the meat, capture wild turkeys, clear land to plant, while mother spins and weaves, makes bread and a zillion other things along with churning butter. The pioneer days were days in the United States of young wives and husbands carving out a life in the wilderness with much struggle and sorrow, but also with some people having the kind of memories Laura Ingalls Wilder had of a family life which many would envy today.

There is a need of sharing the work to provide food, shelter, drink, clothing. There is something very special about father digging the garden, making a chicken coop, examining the profitability of keeping rabbits, working in a way that three-year-olds can watch and copy with realistic demonstration before their eyes of just what their father is providing. There is something that can't have a substitute for having the mother be an expert in making a tremendous variety of bread, apple pies, and homemade ice cream. Smelling, watching, helping, tasting, and feeling have no counterpart in growing up with tangible evidence of the needs being provided.

How many people are rationalizing the fact that they are neglecting to make any kind of home at all and failing to spend any time with their children because they are providing more or being fulfilled or doing "good works." It is possible to destroy the family because your home has fallen apart in the name of doing "good works."

There is a great need to stop as a family together, pray for a whole evening, for a whole day off together, discuss, pray and ask God, "Please show us before it is too late what balance we are to have in our family."

I can say positively that the years fly past like a mist in the night. Time disappears more quickly than smoke. It is not possible to go backward. The "now" is important if there is ever to be any family life. Steve Turner, a young English poet, has a line in his poem "Ageing" which I would like to quote from the book *Tonight We Will Fake Love:*

At some point in his life
There came a shortage
of future

Apply to the family life this truth concerning time. Economic short-ages can never compare with "a shortage of future."

If economic matters are pushing you apart rather than drawing you together, spend some time thinking and praying about it. Two people with two separate careers and living in one house but infre-quently together—with children who are more frequently cared for by other people than by their parents—have really not formed a fam-ily, and the economic things have become a kind of people-eating monster taking all the humanness out of the relationships. What a cold thing is a check for the poor little rich child if it is the only thing that either parent has ever made for him or her. If affluence is the only goal—no matter what—the family will be completely lost.

Whatever is to be said about family economics, small children earning their first money should have the attitude and excitement bred into them from early talking about how to share the family money.

A tenth or other portion will naturally be put aside into another matchbox—or different little bag or wee purse—something to distinguish it as "treasure" which the Lord has commanded us to save. That really is the only savings which the Lord has commanded. But I don't believe He has commanded against having a portion in the barn or bank or storehouse here. It is like the matter of loving the Lord more than father and mother and children, wife and husband, sister and brother, being made emphatic. We are strongly told we are to love each other with a reality that is to be carefully demonstrated. Because we love the Lord more, we will not love each other less; because we give to those with whom the Lord would have us share economically, we will not have less in the end.

ELEVEN
Cheerful Givers

The idea of clothing having an effect on human relationships is not just a matter of getting out of hot, sticky things in warm weather and thus becoming comfortable. How we are dressed has an effect on the way other people treat us. People going to apply for jobs, going to meet the boss, going to meet their girl's parents, or getting ready for any kind of meeting in which they want to make an impression make themselves what they consider to be presentable. Why? Because people do form opinions from first impressions and connect what a person looks like with what they are. Opinions change, of course, but no matter how long we know each other, the matter of how we look and what we wear affects other people's attitudes toward us and has something to do with their treatment of us.

I don't think it is a superficial kind of thing to realize that if you have appeared in the same old thing day after day it is adding strain to other strains. As a wife you should set aside some time to get a different kind of outfit altogether—before the evening meal or for lunch or whatever time the family is going to be together.

Don't think that it is only important to wear attractive things for your husband; it is also important to wear attractive things for your children. Children will behave differently toward an attractively dressed mother just as a husband will.

Strangely enough, even though you are the mother, you will be more polite to your own children if you dress them attractively, just as you will look at yourself in the mirror with more

respect if you splash cold water on your face, redo your hair, and put on something fresh. You can feel like a different person as well as act like a different person when you care and do something about your appearance.

I have always noticed that people traveling with children who are dressed neatly and carrying interesting dolls, cars, or blocks in a bag are not as annoying to people but are looked at with sympathy and interest. People so easily get annoyed with straggly looking children dressed in an assortment of unsuitable clothes when they are on a train or a boat or in a restaurant.

Children dressed in their best clothes are apt to eat with better manners, so I have noticed, than when dressed in their old play clothes. Somehow, clothes do have an effect on human behavior, and this should be taken into account when teaching good manners.

It is good to accept the fact that the whole family will treat each other differently if they are dressed for the occasion, whatever the occasion may be.

Commonsense Christian living is based on knowing that there is nothing as simple in life as a "stable" home composed of people who have no physical difficulties that would spoil the "quality of life." It doesn't take much thinking to realize that a perfect baby at birth can have an accident at six years old, or have polio or another illness at three, which changes the "perfection." What then?

Every parent has the need to study the basic question of how to raise children to be human beings who are not self-centered, but who are considerate, thoughtful, kind, and sensitive to other people's needs. Selfishness develops easily, with the attention on "me, me, me." To have children turn their imagination and thoughts on someone else's pleasures and needs because their brother or sister is handicapped is to prepare them for a growing unselfishness in their lives ahead in this world as it really is.

Some months ago Debby and Udo told me of a fellow who was living in Chalet Gentiana with them. "We noticed," Debby said, "how very considerate he was. He noticed little things and jumped up to get things for people, and he was so kind and thoughtful with children. One day I asked him, 'Could you tell me why you are so different from most young people? You really are so considerate.'"

His answer was one that each parent of a handicapped child should listen to carefully. "I guess it is because we have a Down's syndrome sister. We other children always thought of what we could do for her so that she wouldn't be left out, . . . how we could take care of some need for her and encourage her. You know, we all love her very much and so it was genuine interest in her happiness. I guess it has made us more aware of other people in general."

A "normal" home, a "stable" home? This boy has been raised in the best kind of home . . . a home with a handicapped sister whom the parents had carefully taught the brothers to care for and to include. Human beings were growing up in that home with an unselfishness rarely found in the twentieth century.

To care for someone's special needs, to use imagination as to what might be done to include the boy or girl in various activities, is not a hindrance for the other children but an open door to invention and originality as well as to developing kindness and patience.

If a child is not where the others are mentally, and a game like dominoes is being played, a set of special dominoes for small children with animals and fruit or flowers to be matched can be going on at once, and turns can be taken as to which game each one is part of. There are games in which cards are matched. There are puzzles that are simple. This child can be helped to do the puzzle with as much help and enthusiasm as is needed, while a more complicated thousand-piece jigsaw puzzle is being put together by the others.

Scrapbooks can be made by your other children with pictures that would interest her or him and some pages with textures to feel—like velvet, satin, rough wool. Stimulation is always needed.

When the family story is being read, one of the other children can be placing pictures on a felt board or a magnetic board much as one would amuse another child at church. The very fact of being together is important for everyone. And stimulating the imagination of your children as to what might be helpful educationally or as a pleasure is a plus in the growth of that personality, not a minus.

It is old-fashioned to talk about character building these days, but that is really what it is all about. Figuring out how someone who is all "locked in" to his handicapped body can have a little more freedom is a challenge that is helpful to character building of the whole family if the attitude is what it should be.

We are talking about commonsense Christian living. It is a very special contrast to talk to the loving brothers and sisters of the "locked in" child and to remind them that one day in the future the body will be perfect in a twinkling of an eye when Jesus comes back. Then there will not be a shred of a handicap, but physical and mental and emotional and spiritual perfection. What a contrast. And how great that it is true!

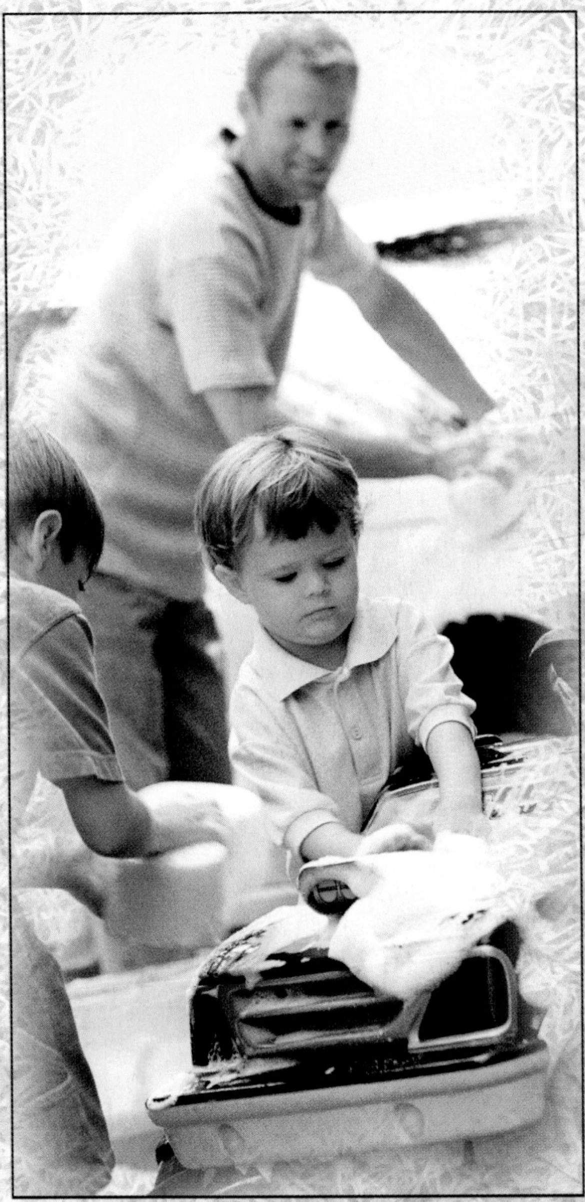

The popular opinion of a relationship, expressed in all the media, is that it is something that should provide fulfillment, satisfaction, happiness, enjoyment, pleasure, understanding, and contentment. How quickly must all these positive things take place in a relationship? In the "now." All too often the immediate moment's desire or hunger tempts us all to make an incredible exchange.

Do you remember Esau's choice? Esau sold his birthright, which meant affecting human beings for generations to come. He threw away a precious possibility of a different life for himself and his children and children's children, right down to the descendants of Esau today. Percussions, consequences, ripples in history still going on today were affected by Esau's choice at that time. Human beings are *not* pebbles that fall into the water and cause no ripple. Our choices cause unending ripples. Esau chose to satisfy his immediate hunger as the fumes from a red lentil stew hit his nostrils. What an exchange for a birthright!

But day after day, thousands of people choose a totally selfish search for personal happiness. Some, for immediate fulfillment, choose freedom to do what feels good or to kick anyone who might get in the way. They exchange continuity for one's self and for one's children and grandchildren for a terrific variety of that "mess of pottage." What "mess of pottage" has tempted you or me, and how can we see things clearly in the light of the *whole* history rather than in the immediate *now*?

FOURTEEN

Living Patterns

When children hear a constant barrage of "I want my rights," "I want happiness," "I want to do my own thing," "I want to go out and get what I deserve in life," "I want to be fulfilled," "I want the perfect relationship," they are constantly being taken into the area of daydreams—selfish, egotistical daydreams. Perfection does *not* exist. There are no perfect people or perfect situations. Your or my "rights" collide head-on with another person's "rights."

Facing the reality of being imperfect—explaining to children that the family is made up of a number of imperfect people of different ages, living together under often difficult circumstances—puts things into perspective.

There is an oft-repeated statement these days: "Children are better off if their parents divorce, because a home where there are fights and constant disagreements is very bad for them." What is ignored all too often is the fact that children discuss with other children the signs of an impending divorce, and what terrifies them and brings tears in the night is the fear that the fights they are overhearing mean a split is on the way.

No one of any age feels comfortable when people are shouting at each other, but there is a measure of comfort in being assured that although this disagreement may sound fierce, there *will be* a solution. One of the two who are arguing will have enough imagination and ingenuity to work out a solution concerning "the day off" or "the vacation" about which there is a difference of opinion!

Children need to be able to say to other children, "Well, my mom and dad get a little upset at times. One or the other gets very angry at other times. But they do love each other really, and they love us, and they have lots of imagination and many ideas as to how to make it all up and do something pleasant together after the fight is over."

There is a desperate need for loving patterns of how to cope, not just seminars on the subject. There is a need of seeing a compromise work out in a real-life situation. There is great value in hearing someone keep quiet or in watching patience work! The skill of changing the subject without doing so obnoxiously needs to be observed.

Children need to *see* solutions take place, not only as a reassuring factor in their present home lives but as an example for the future.

Sadly, very few children today have seen the pattern of living through differences, coming out on the other side of them, of someone's apologizing to someone else—or both apologizing—and then one of the two having a brainstorm about going for a picnic, eating supper in front of the fire, having watermelon under the lilac bushes, playing a game after supper, reading two chapters of the current book while nibbling on popcorn, or getting out a map and planning a "someday kind of vacation." And very few children have friends who can tell them how it works.

49

"I have struggled for years with a problem regarding one of my three children for whom I do not have a feeling of love," one mother lamented. Her problem is not unusual. It is not possible to have exactly the same kind of feelings toward each of your children. There are differences of personality between parents and children. Each child is an individual personality, a human being, and no two are alike.

I have heard a mother saying after her first child was a few years old, "I know how to bring up a child. This is the way to do it." After a second and third child came along, that same mother confessed she had spoken too soon. The children's reactions were so different, and her problems changed her assurance that she had hit upon exactly the right formula.

Sometimes the third or the fourth child is the easiest one. For others it is the first child who is the easiest to understand and to enjoy. Then comes the unexpected shock of stubbornness or lack of response from the second child to the same series of things that brought pleasure to the first.

Children can irritate a parent at times. There are a variety of things they can do to irritate a parent. Being too loud or too silent, too perfectionistic or too careless, too energetic or too lazy. You alone know what irritates you; perhaps you just feel fussy without analyzing the cause.

Try to discover what the irritating things are when they take place. What are the things that make you feel the "I could shake her until she is jelly" kind of feelings or bring the "I can't stand this anymore" kind of pressure? Find out *when* this happens and how often. Is there a time when it does *not* happen? Contrast the times when you have been totally unfair because of your overreaction and when you have been reasonable and calm.

Now review your child's greatest interest, his greatest talent. What is the thing that needs encouraging and enhancing in his personality? Give your attention to thinking about this growing human being you are influencing.

Forget that this is a child you are supposed to love and for whom you are trying to conjure up the proper feeling, and think of him or her as a friend—perhaps an irritating one, but one you want to get to know better.

Try to find a beginning spot, something you can do together. Would she love a ballet? Find a classical ballet, if such exists near you, and surround it with a good time of enjoying each other's reactions. The talking will open up later. Real communication can't be forced. In due course you will find you have enjoyed her as a person.

Ask the God of love, who is his God as well as yours, not to allow that child to be deprived of the richness he could have in having your love. Pray hour by hour for a measure of love for him that hour. Then ask specifically for the reality of love to come to you as a surprise in the midst of doing what God has outlined as the thing love does do.

First Corinthians 13:4–7 says,

> Love is patient, love is kind. It does not envy, it does not boast, it is not proud. It is not rude, it is not self-seeking, it is not easily angered, it keeps no record of wrongs. Love does not delight in evil but rejoices with the truth. It always protects, always trusts, always hopes, always perseveres.

Point by point, use your imagination to figure out ways to practically practice love as defined by God. There are two things to do:

First, love is patient. You can be patient with your child. You can bite your tongue and stop the words of criticism or sharp retort because something annoys you, and you can be patient in the midst of things you can't stand.

Second, love is kind. That is an outward thing you can do. You can do something kind for him. As you do an outwardly kind thing, you are expressing to him what God says love is even if you don't have the wave of warm feeling inside.

In the midst of trying to get to know your child as a person and also of trying to follow the reality of what God says love consists of, it seems to me that slowly and surely the feelings of love will come.

W hat is the cause that brings an effect into the place where it is seen, smelled, touched, heard, felt? Where do actions originate?

In the mind. Just as creativity is in the mind first, so devastating destruction is in the mind first. Violence is in the mind first.

Ideas come first.

Ideas matter.

Ideas give birth to action—good or bad.

Ideas give people their worldview.

Ideas push people into heroism.

Ideas drive people into vandalism.

Ideas are meant to be handed down from generation to generation. People are not born as finished products. Teaching and instruction, the passing on of ideas, takes place whether it is true or false teaching.

Discussion of truth with the next generation is not just a rote memorization but discussion of ideas while hiking in the woods, walking along a city street, sitting by a fireside or at the kitchen table, or at bedtime. This is an admonition to give the next generation a base for action developed on the existence of God, and a real putting first of a love for God and then action based on love for other human beings.

One generation is responsible for the next. Whoever is doing the planting of ideas—the parents, or teachers, or professors in universities—may live a life of actions based on another's teaching. That is, it is quite possible for people to have a personal ethic that does not belong to what they are teaching the next generation. They are then surprised and even dismayed when the next generation, their own pupils, begin carrying out in action what they have been given in the realm of ideas in action.

You might contemplate the effect of Hegel's relativism on Hitler's ideas. Think of Hegel's effect on Hitler's ideas in the realm of providing a base for Hitler's actions. People do open doors for following generations—down into the depths of despair for thinking young people, down into drastic action for others. Suicide follows some, cruelty to other people follows others. Ideas and philosophies don't just end up in people's minds or on the pages of books but in the actions of individual lives and nations.

The people who bear responsibility for the actions taken in different periods of history are those who inject ideas into the minds of the young.

Time spent alone with your children should be time not simply spent teaching them another Sunday school lesson. Time should be taken to have a meal together, to go to a place that is a treat for them—a park, a beach, a lake boat, a Mississippi riverboat, a walk down a country lane—whatever is available to you where you live. In a year's time something should be included in the area of the arts—concerts, ballets, art museums. You may live near Boston or St. Louis or London, or Paris or Zurich or Minneapolis. The possibilities are different depending on where you live.

When Fran was a pastor in St. Louis, Sunday was his busiest day of the week, with four services at the church. Therefore, Monday was his day off. As soon as the older girls were out of school in the afternoon we'd go with the three girls to the St. Louis Art Museum. This is a good place for children to go from one room to the other, always finding adequate space to sit down and draw in front of a painting or a sculpture.

There was an atmosphere in that museum conducive to children having the privilege to walk until they saw something they wanted to try drawing, then to sit in front of it and look for a long time. Fran would say, "Sit still and look at that picture and tell me what you see. You can't really see it when you just walk past." He would teach them to appreciate art.

Then we would go on to a place in the park called "The Jewel Box," a greenhouse full of plants and flowers with a little fountain. We would go and sit in the cool, fragrant atmosphere, look at the flowers, talk about them, notice the changes in the displays as the season changed. The greenhouse was part of their lives, but it was also an important part of the three girls being treated as important. It gave time for some serious answering of questions along the way or for simply enjoying the beauty of God's creativity together.

Christian parents have an imperative, a really urgent need to introduce their children to the kind of things that will go with them all through life, natural responses to and appreciation of beauty. During these experiences you are getting to know your children and really treating them as human beings worth sharing good memories with. As you introduce them to an enjoyment of beauty of sight and sound, of taste and smell, in this setting your conversation about God is not artificial. You are taking seriously the fact that people are made in the image of the Creator.

I f creative projects are to follow one after another there must be a balance of priorities. A clean and orderly house is a joy to everyone, yet there is a need to be sensitive to the greater importance of freedom to paint, mix clay, scatter pieces of clothing in cutting a dress or a sail. The possibility of getting soil on a waxed floor is far less important than the wonder of a tiny box with an exciting mix of green showing that the plants are coming up. Cotton stuffing for a wobbly sewn cotton or wool animal can be in danger of scattering wisps of fluff over the couch, but there is a moment when the four-year-old's help in pushing in the cotton for the eight-year-old's elephant must be recognized as the high point of her day. The priorities mustn't get mixed up. An atmosphere conducive to creativity must be one of respect for the young artist—however talented or clumsy the attempt has been—respect for the need of making a mess.

Creativity needs an audience, some appreciation, the response of another human being, as well as the freedom to be accomplished and some raw materials to work with. It may be easy enough to hang the drawings and paintings of a small child, to make a shelf for the early rough shapes formed in clay, to provide a temporary museum for their collection of shells, stones, leaves, butterflies or bugs, stamps or buttons. However, to stop your work and be an audience may seem a nuisance or just too inconvenient.

Be sensitive to the need of bringing your phone conversation to a close, putting your book aside, deciding on an easier dessert for supper, stopping your cleaning chores. With perhaps some knitting in hand, come and sit and watch the "all important" circus, wedding, play, concert, set of magic tricks, reading of an original book, play of an event in history. No matter how clumsy the production is, this long planned or suddenly put together event needs audience appreciation and reaction.

Creativity needs the availability of reaching the attention of a sympathetic friend at just the right moment. Someone needs to come and watch, listen, look, respond. If there is helpful criticism to be given, the first flush of excited completion of a work is not the moment to give it. A good rule to remember is that right after the baby song, play, or picture has been presented, anything you say must be positive.

An atmosphere of trust brings forth a sharing of ideas and an attempt to make things, with an expectation that the most wonderful thing is about to come forth. This atmosphere comes if the basic attitude is one which takes mistakes and fresh attempts as quite expected. "Oops! But I am sure the kite will work well if we put a bit of tail on it."

The inspiration of freedom, communication, and trust needs the example of adult creativity within the family. Each parent should be doing his own thing in music, painting, dressmaking, tailoring, furniture making, curtain making, the sewing of bits of leftover pieces together to make quilts, writing, flower and vegetable gardening, producing a fantastic garden in a huge bottle, baking bread, branching out in all sorts of fresh ways of cooking as an art.

There should also be an example of how creativity can be a way of expressing love. Simple gestures of thoughtfulness bring forth natural and spontaneous creative acts on the part of everyday life.

God put the first family in inspiring surroundings. As much as possible each family should prepare a home with as much to inspire as possible.

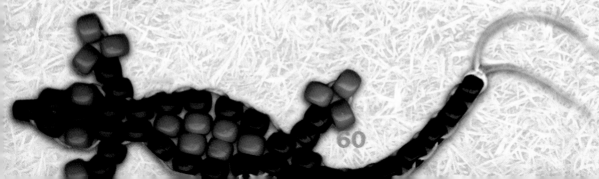

NINETEEN

Encouraging Independence

Discovery needs some guidance and instruction and preparation by wise and imaginative parents, so that many things are learned in various areas of everyday life.

You introduce your children to discovery when you expose them to finger paints, or tempera paints and a brush, or modeling clay or a dish of dough. Opening discovery includes introducing children to one step when the next step can be totally original—trying something out for the first time.

It is a "being allowed to discover what it is like" affair in a variety of areas—without mother saying: "You're too young to make a dress. Here, hem this handkerchief." I remember when I was nine, I made my first dress. Admittedly, it was extremely simple—like a doll dress, a front and a back with raglan sleeves. I laboriously put bias binding around the neck and sleeve by hand. The stitches were crooked, but I wore the dress proudly.

Let your young son discover what it is like to make muffins. When he is older he will be able to follow a recipe. Boys need to learn to cook as much as girls. Tell him that most of the chefs in the famous restaurants of the world are men. As you get out the mixing bowl and ingredients, you grit your teeth and say to yourself, "This is going to be a mess, but I want him to do it himself." Then you say aloud, "Go ahead and break the egg in that bowl. That's right. Oops! Never mind, we'll get another one. Here."

You point out what comes next in a simple recipe for muffins. "Go ahead, measure it in this cup. Now put this in and then that. Now stir it up with this big spoon. Take this margarine and grease the muffin pans like this. See?"

The first jam I ever made alone was peach conserve. Let your children discover what it is like to put peaches in boiling water to loosen the skins, to carefully lift them out one at a time with a slotted spoon and when cooled a bit to see the skin peel off like magic. Let them cut up two or three cupfuls of peaches and add an equal amount of sugar, a couple of handfuls of raisins, a teaspoon of cinnamon, and stir it as it boils to a proper thickness. It will be their first peach conserve and can be enjoyed later in the week . . . a discovery that canning and making jelly and jam last longer than the making of one meal.

My mother let me pour paraffin in a tin can to carefully pour over the conserve to preserve it. I had the fun (which I still remember) of watching the paraffin gradually cool and harden into a white seal. That seal was not to be broken until we wanted to eat the peach conserve on fresh hot biscuits, which I had then learned to make by myself. I still remember my satisfaction.

Children should not have everything done *for* them, so that all they learn to do is push buttons on an electronic game.

One of the easiest ways of promoting an atmosphere of discussion and reading and music in the household is to prohibit much television watching. If you want to have family life that is conducive to really talking and exchanging ideas, listening to music on the stereo, discussing or reading about the composer and the musicians, and then reading books aloud together is a must as far as I am concerned. Educating the children to enjoy a great variety of books being read aloud opens doors to reading current events and discussing opinions as a natural part of family life.

The hour of reading by the fireplace, or out in the sunshine, or in a boat . . . educating children to look forward to the family reading aloud together is essential for a great many reasons. As a substitute for TV, it is one of the most important things that can be done. It is hard to include in the day, but it should take precedence over other things.

In our family, not only did I read many hours with each of my children, and together at certain times of their lives, but they are now reading to their children. At reading time in Greatham when Ranald and Susan are busy with L'Abri work and at reading time in Chalet Gentiana when Debby and Udo are busy with their work the moment comes when

TWENTY

Joys of Reading

the word is: "Sorry, this is the reading hour for our children." It is not a time for neglecting other people who come to L'Abri for help. Rather it is a giving of the best demonstration they could possibly have of what family life is all about. It is not "putting on a demonstration" like an act. It is simply letting people get a glimpse of the pattern of family life.

When it comes to news that will be on TV, I would say watch it together and then discuss it. Have the newspaper read aloud if there is time; or if you have read it separately, discuss various things. "This is slanted." "This article is reporting news with an editorial opinion trying to change opinion among readers." Then, of course, when you read what you consider good reporting or a good editorial, read it and praise it, and say why it is good.

Introduce your children to international and national news, and help them to think about it and learn to modify what they are getting. This is a portion of what will make your home an educational supplement to whatever they are getting at school. These lessons learned at home will be valuable to them all their lives.

Can you protect your child from everything, from all the threats around you in your particular "neck of the woods"? Can you foresee every temptation and prepare him or her for that? Were your parents and grandparents at different moments in history able to achieve the unfolding of a perfect childhood as they cared for you or for your parents?

No, there is not, and never has been, a golden age for children. As we live in this moment of history, we need to use our own common sense. We need to pray for the wisdom of the Lord beyond our own. We need to do all that we can possibly do within the "circle of possibilities" not to allow children to become "extinct" because of the pollution of the media, malls, and schools—the great variety of poison that is designed to do away with any possibility of hopscotch, rope-jumping, hide-and-seek, tree climbing, walking on stilts, fishing, rowboating, campfire cooking, imaginatively discovering childhood.

There is discovery that is ghastly—discovery of drugs at the age of eight or nine, discovery of alcoholism at ten or eleven, discovery of sex and pregnancy at eleven or twelve. These discoveries are ones by which human beings are actually making money, polluting and wiping out the childhood of little human beings.

One of our most important goals in commonsense Christian living should be to do something for our children, and for other children in preserving this thing called childhood, which is rapidly growing extinct. In some circles it is a meaningless word.

65

TWENTY-TWO

Discipline God's Way

The discipline of children in a Christian home needs to be combined with the recognition of the discipline of the parents by the Word of God. In other words, nobody should attempt in a Christian home to discipline their children without remembering that we are under discipline too—the discipline of the Word of God. We don't make up the rules ourselves.*

We need to remember a number of things. For one, a father is not to drive his child crazy. There is to be gentleness and kindness just as our Heavenly Father is gentle and kind. We need to remember that God gives us the picture of His being there, ready to catch us when we fall, even as an eagle flies under the young eaglets. God says His wings are under us. In some way we need to demonstrate this aspect of being in the right place at the right time when we as parents are needed. We are to be counted upon, trusted to understand.

When I see a child fall and hear a parent say, "Oh, you awkward thing, look at your new dress," as he or she jerks the little one by the arm, I think of the gentleness of God the Father picking us up when we fall into sin, a temptation, a mistake, a foolish choice. We parents need to remember that we are the representation to our children of the word "father" and the reality of what a father is.

Of course, I am talking of mothers too. God speaks in His Word to mothers many times. The love and wisdom of a mother is an important part of the growing-up days.

* See Edith Schaeffer, *Ten Things Parents Must Teach Their Children (And Learn for Themselves)* (Grand Rapids: Baker Book House, 1994).

It is incredible when you consider how much a human being learns in the first two years of life . . . and from that moment until he is plunged into all that our culture surrounds him with. The time is short for teaching the basics on the basis of truth and love. Mothers also need to sit under the Word of God.

> In your struggle against sin, you have not yet resisted to the point of shedding your blood. And you have forgotten that word of encouragement that addresses you as sons.
>
> > "My sons, do not make light of the Lord's discipline,
> >   and do not lose heart when he rebukes you,
> > because the Lord disciplines those he loves,
> >   and he punishes everyone he accepts as a son."
>
> Endure hardship as discipline; God is treating you as sons. For what son is not disciplined by his father? If you are not disciplined (and everyone undergoes discipline), then you are illegitimate children and not true sons.
>
> Hebrews 12:4–8

The passage goes on to say that we have all had human fathers who have disciplined us as they thought best, but God disciplines us so that we may share in His holiness. It is specifically for our good. There are no mistakes.

> No discipline seems pleasant at the time, but painful. Later on, however, it produces a harvest of righteousness and peace for those who have been trained by it.
>
> Hebrews 12:11

I am not saying that there should not be discipline. To say that would contradict the teaching God gives us in the Bible. However, we are not God, and we need to ask for help in all our choices in life. Unhappily, an angry or frustrated and very annoyed parent is not usually in the mood to quietly pray for an idea as to the best punishment for the deed. We all do make mistakes. Happily, we don't have to pretend to our children that we have always been perfect, and we can take time to go back and admit our mistakes.

Be very careful, and remember that the time to prepare to be careful is when you are alone and thinking. It is harder in the midst of chaos. The discipline should be decisive and adequate, but not too much for the misdeed. Differentiate between a genuine mistake and a deliberate deed. Be careful that the reason for the punishment is understood by the child. Patience is part of it. Again, what is love? Love suffers long and is kind. Love has patience. Make sure love is displayed in the context of the discipline, and afterwards, in being kind.

Children and adults react differently in emotional, spiritual, intellectual, and psychological areas when there is some special physical need. Not only does someone in the family have to be cognizant of this fact, but someone needs to take responsibility. What am I talking about? Blood sugar level dropping, hunger pangs, fatigue, clothing, cleanliness, great heat or devastating cold, pleasant or unpleasant flavors, noise.

David comes home from school, cold and cranky because his blood sugar level is low, tired from a long day. This is not the time to say, "Go right over now and apologize to Mr. X next door for the broken window. It was your ball game. I don't care if you threw it or not. And then get right back here and do your homework." Is not the impolite answer which David spits back partly due to his physical condition?

Your understanding of the human frame ought to make you start out by saying, "Here, David, come and drink the hot chocolate (or vanilla eggnog or milkshake) along with some of my homemade brown bread and peanut butter. Isn't it good? Your pants and socks are wet from the snow. Why don't you take a hot shower and get into these dry things right away." After David feels like a new person, full tummy, warm and dry, then the suggestion may be received with a different attitude and the homework tackled with some feeling of being able to face it.

Your toddler and four-year-old are fussing and whining. Nothing seems to suit them. Your understanding of the way bodies work should remind you that they, as well as adults, have lowered blood sugar when they get hungry. Not only is food needed,

71

but something soothing and calming. Daddy will be home soon, and what a disaster is about to happen (with scoldings and cryings imminent) as a bad beginning to an evening.

What to do? Pop the two in a bath, a lovely hot one if it has been a cold day, a cool one if it has been a hot summer evening, some mild bubbles or a lovely smelling bath oil, a few floating toys. They'll be in a different mood in a few minutes, and you can finish your last minute preparations for supper. Take care of the hunger problem right then and there, unless you are certain that the supper table won't disintegrate into squabbling. Put the four-year-old in bed with a tray adorned with a few flowers, a candle in a stable little holder, scrambled eggs and toast, yogurt or a bit of whatever you are making yourself. Feed the baby on your lap as the little one eats, or do the whole thing in your kitchen. It can be varied at different times, but don't have Daddy always meet the little ones at the moment when they are the fussiest due to fatigue, hunger, plus feeling too hot or too cold or too uncomfortable.

Adults who disintegrate into ogres yelling, "You must obey me," to little people who don't know why they feel so "unable to get hold of themselves," and thus feel and act worse and worse, ought to use common sense to think of the fact that there are times when the basic needs of food, a freshening up with a bath, clean clothes, and a rest are needed before the commands are given.

M any children have gone berserk, if I could put it that way, from being given too-high standards and by being treated as if they would have to be perfect to please you . . . no matter how imperfect you parents are as people! You live out your imperfections in daily life. We all do. To be fair to children, your (our) imperfections must be a subject of conversation. You must say without hesitation that no one is perfect, and that, of course, you are *really* imperfect.

"Look at little John Lewis. He's being imperfect right now. He has been told not to touch the sound system, and he is touching it while he is saying 'Don't touch! Don't touch!'" We have an overwhelming appreciation of imperfection at times. It is so interesting in a brand-new person. Then all of a sudden it hits us the wrong way and we reach out and whack!

Is there to be no discipline then? Yes, of course there is to be discipline—but fair, even discipline, recognizing that no one is going to achieve perfection until Jesus comes back again and we're all changed to be perfect.

Discipline is to teach a child acceptable behavior or to protect against terrible dangers like being burned or hit by a truck. To expect perfection is not only unrealistic, but totally unfair in teaching the truth of what the abnormal world is like and what human beings are.

I would rather put aside discipline than have the child think that I thought I was always perfect. Bitterness has come among the children of Christians when they have received what they felt was totally unfair treatment. They were punished for things they observed their parents doing, or for behaving in ways they observed their parents behaving.

It is important to say to children when it is true, "Look, I did something that was really wrong. I'm awfully sorry. I lost my cool. I lost my temper. I got mad. I shouted about something I should not have shouted about. I realize that you were just being creative over there, while I was concentrating on something I was composing. Your music clashed with my notes." You need to say something to put it into the context of reality and life. Their lives are not going to be easier than yours. They need your help.

There must be no pressure for perfection when perfection is not possible. We all put pressure somewhere, and we need to be careful to evaluate the fairness of the pressure our demands are causing. As we try to be balanced our attitude must be, "Here are imperfect children, and here are two imperfect parents. We are going to spend a certain portion of our lives in the same home. After that comes whatever—the career, the wedding day, the study and travel—and never again are we going to live the same way under the same roof."

Paul is speaking to children when he says, "Children obey your parents in the Lord, for this is right" (Ephesians 6:1). But in the same chapter he strongly cautions parents: "Fathers, do not exasperate your children; instead bring them up in the training and instruction of the Lord" (v. 4).

There needs to be time for careful examination day by day as to what you might be doing to exasperate your children and turn them away from both you and the Lord, rather than giving them excitement and interest in pursuing truth.

One way of having the right kind of influence on our children is by making it clear that we are all together in the same boat of being imperfect but that we may have help. Nobody is perfect but the Triune God. Nobody else is. However, as a family living with the desire to obey what God wants us to be, we don't expect to follow the lead of unbelieving people around us any more than the Israelites were expected to follow the standards, customs, and lifestyles of the Baal worshipers living around them. We expect our family to be different and we expect each other to be different . . . even if not perfect.

One other thing needs to be said in answer to this question. Don't forget to give praise and appreciation to your children. People have told me that their parents never praised them no matter what marks they got in school. The report card was always met with, "You could have done better." People of all ages need encouragement. Children need praise and acclaim from their parents for tiny performances as well as great ones.

Unfair pressure often comes through trying to reach the expectations of others rather than dealing directly before the Lord with plain good common sense as to what is important for the child at that particular point in his or her life.

Let me illustrate. The first of August is the Swiss National Independence Day—a day of old-fashioned bonfires, patriotic parades and speeches, and fireworks. When Franky was a small boy, each village family had their own fireworks. Franky always asked if he could collect money for the fireworks. Now L'Abri had a principle of praying for financial needs rather than asking for money, but this wasn't money for L'Abri; it was a little boy's desire to put on a great production! Our answer was "yes." He asked for contributions from people who would be enjoying the production. Our conviction was that this was an important occasion to Franky, and that all the people certainly got their money's worth. When he had collected the freewill contributions for the celebration, he went off happily to the store in Villars and made his careful selection.

Then came the day itself. Year after year Franky made great preparations. He nailed pinwheels to plum trees and put up elaborate wooden frames for various kinds of fountains and so forth to be fastened at different heights. There were rockets laid out in a neat row as the time approached, and various other interesting affairs. Franky had also marked places for the wheelchairs of the children at Bellevue, the cerebral palsy home next door, and benches for all the L'Abri people and the workers, therapists, and nurses in Bellevue. My part was to make enough cakes and ice cream for everyone.

The audience was satisfied and excited as they listened to the master of ceremonies. Franky himself announced each event. They watched the display, knowing there would be homemade ice cream and a selection of cake after the grand finale. As many as 135 people enjoyed the widened family time, talking of climbers who were lighting flares on the tops of the mountains and thanking Franky for his earnest hard work to make the evening's memory unforgettable.

Now it was approaching the first of August one year when Franky was about seven or eight years old. His usual box with the hole in the top had been taken from person to person throughout the day, and he was listening to the jingle with obvious satisfaction.

I was in the Chalet les Melezes kitchen doing dishes with a young man who was bitter and superior about Christianity. He had come from a Christian home and had gone to a Christian college, but he had turned away from it all. Suddenly he whirled around from the place where he stood drying dishes and spoke to me: "It seems to me that you [and the *you* was spoken with a sarcastic sneer] ought to stop your boy from collecting money for fireworks. You ought to send that money to the *heathen* . . . to preach the gospel." I can't express the kind of sneering malice that came forth from his voice.

I whirled around from the sink and spoke with just as much emphasis in my voice, I hope not a sneer, but I am afraid I was strong and not sweet, as I said, "If your parents had let you collect money for fireworks, and let you put on the kind of production Franky does, perhaps you wouldn't be against Christianity as you are."

Money has a variety of special uses to provide memories and beauty and fulfillment of creativity on the part of children. The "preaching of the gospel" will be helped more by giving your children a rich and full childhood than by sternly sitting them in a chair and giving them lectures. Please remember that I really believe in sharing the gospel with the lost, food with the hungry, and clothing with the poor, and in teaching children to have compassion, but it all has its proper place in the balance.

You have just vacuumed the living room rug, and the hall is spic-and-span; now you can turn to the next thing on your list. Suddenly the door bursts open and little Susie or Johnny comes in happily with a fistful of dandelions and early spring violets with a few blades of grass and weeds mixed in. His or her eyes are full of delight, sparkling with assurance of bringing love in that grubby hand, expectant of a welcome for this treasured arrangement. Mud is mixed with leaves and dry blades of grass, as sandals or boots leave a trail across the clean rug. The outstretched hand is accompanied by a breathless, "Look, Mommy, for you."

What is going on inside? It started out in the garden or field, that sudden idea, that original burst of imagination which pictured a communication of love with the gift. This is a little three-year-old's budding understanding of giving some material evidence of a hard-to-put-into-words feeling. This is an important moment, long to be remembered, later to be added to with fresh understanding.

What is the response?

"Susie [or Johnny], how lovely! You picked those for Mommy, didn't you? Let's find a vase for them. They will be put right on Mommy's bedside table to remind her that you thought of her when you were playing." The child has a warm feeling of success in communicating. Mommy understands what is going on. Perhaps there is a verbalization now—"I love you, Mommy." Or perhaps just a turning to go out again, secure in a growing relationship. Then, as the child leaves the doorstep, a suggestion is made: "Next time, dear, try to remember to come in the kitchen door." After all, how long will it take to brush up mud and leaves, to whiz the vacuum cleaner over a few spots again? How expensive is this as a price to pay for responding to love with understanding?

Or is this what happens?

"Susie [or Johnny], you little monster! Look at all the mud and those dirty leaves and stuff on my clean rugs. Get out of here with your nasty weeds; I'm getting ready for company. How many times do I have to tell you to come in the kitchen door!" All this is accompanied by a rough shake and a shove toward the door. The light dies out of the child's eyes, the tousled head drops down in confusion, tears drip silently or with audible weeping, depending on the child. Something has been so thoroughly stepped on, squashed, hurt, that the withered drying of the little bunch of weedy flowers is only a picture of the worse withering taking place inside the child. What a costly price to pay for gaining the feeling of, "Well, I told the child off. He [she] will remember the next time to do what I say. I don't vacuum rugs for nothing. I'm not to be imposed upon and made into a slave by my children."

Whichever response, a lesson has been given and learned concerning human relationships. Something has been taught more vividly than any lecture could teach it. An opportunity has been used—one way or another. It is not neutral.

The parent may be self-satisfied with the feeling, "I've told him off now. Let's see how he likes it. He won't dirty up my house again." But that parent might be amazed that the rebellion of ten years later has had its seed sown in that moment. That parent might be horrified that the inhumane treatment a thirty-three-year-old is one day going to give to another human being is being prepared for at this very time.

"What can possibly be the far-reaching effect of one incident?" True, one time is not sufficient to finish the job, but a succession of "one times" adds up, especially if there is no apology given, no verbalized recognition that you have been thoughtless and rude. Neglected mothers and grandmothers perhaps have been preparing for their own neglect by teaching over and again that people's sensitive feelings and people's need of response are never as important as clean houses, schedules, rules, and regulations.